Dedication to

Colleen Drippé, a great writer and a great friend

A writer's soul is what tethers the story to the reader. It is the voice that cries out from the characters.

–NATHANIEL CONNORS

Contents

INTRODUCTION

Owning Your Voice

Writing a book about author voice? I get the irony.

If voice is personal and distinctive—something that grows out of who you are—how can anyone teach it? Isn't that like handing someone a recipe for originality?

I'm not here to teach you how to sound like me. Or like Tolkien, or Terry Pratchett, or whichever author you admire. You don't want that, anyway; readers already have those voices. They want yours. What I want to do is help you recognize the fabulous, one-of-a-kind voice you already have and show you how to refine it intentionally.

Author voice isn't magic. It's not fairy dust sprinkled over a manuscript, nor a gift bestowed after you've written a million words—though the million words certainly help. It is also not something you manufacture by straining to sound literary. In fact, if you force it, it will sound forced.

Voice, rather, comes out of the accumulated result of your choices.

It shows up in the language you gravitate toward and the way your sentences naturally move. Some writers lean into crisp, direct phrases; others prefer layered sentences that unfold gradually. Some linger on physical detail; others focus on emotional nuance or sharp dialogue. Even the way you handle your characters—whether you treat them tenderly, ruthlessly, or with amused detachment—reveals something about your narrative personality.

Over time, those tendencies repeat. They form patterns. And those patterns become recognizable. That's voice.

Readers may not always be able to explain why they know a passage is yours, but they recognize it. (That's why most prolific readers can tell AI-generated content right away.) They feel it in the cadence and tone, in the how worldview permeates the story. That recognition is why readers follow authors across genres.

Voice builds loyalty.

When your voice is steady and consistent, readers relax. They sense that someone competent is guiding them through the story. They know what to expect. For example, I've written parody about redneck space crews or hard science fiction near a black hole, but readers know to expect sound decision making and plot complications that come from events, not people being stupid to advance the plot. That's an aspect of my voice.

When I read Colleen Drippé's work, I know to expect a Classic SF feel, no matter how recent the story. Larry Correia is going to give sound explanations and logical use of weaponry, whether modern-day firearms or alternate-universe magic. Those are integral to their voices. And I know when I'm in the mood for one or the other, I can turn to them to supply it.

Most writers do not struggle with *having* a voice. They struggle with *recognizing* it and shaping it. Comparisons can create insecurity that makes them hesitate. The desire to be correct leads to overediting. Trying to sound impressive or marketable makes the writing stiff until it starts to resemble a written infomercial rather than a living narrative.

Others assume voice is something mystical they either possess or lack, and that belief alone keeps them from developing it. I'm assuming if you have this book, that's not you. Regardless, voice is not mystical. It is craft-informed personality on the page.

That distinction matters. You should absolutely be yourself. At the same time, "be yourself" is incomplete advice. You can be yourself inconsistently. You can be yourself without clarity. You can be yourself in a way that doesn't translate cleanly to the page. Craft makes authenticity readable.

The goal of this book is not to help you invent a persona. It is to help you become so aware of your natural tendencies that you can lean into them deliberately—or adjust them when the story demands it—without losing your core.

That is the difference between accidental voice and developed voice.

We are not going to get into deep meditations on the nature of identity. Let's examine voice in practical terms instead. We'll look at how different authors approach the same material, how genre shapes delivery without erasing individuality, and how author voice differs from character voice. We'll also examine what weakens voice and how to strengthen it through conscious practice.

With reflection questions and exercises, you've got a workshop in book form.

By the end, you will not sound like me. You will sound more like *yourself*—clearer, more confident, and more intentional from the very first page.

So let's begin with the question writers toss around constantly and rarely define: *What is author voice, anyway?*

CHAPTER ONE

What Author Voice Is (and Isn't)

If you ask ten writers to define author voice, you'll get at least twelve answers.

Some will say it's tone. Others will insist it's rhythm. Some people will wave vaguely and call it "style." A few may speak reverently of authenticity, as if it were a rare creature that only appears under the right emotional conditions.

None of those answers are entirely wrong. They're just incomplete.

Before we define voice, let's look at it.

Take four wildly different writers: E.E. Cummings, Dr. Seuss, Sir Arthur Conan Doyle, and J.R.R. Tolkien. You don't need a literature degree to recognize that they don't sound remotely alike.

Cummings refused to capitalize words unless he was referring to God. His poetry looks unconventional before you even read it. The visual presentation is part of his voice. When you do read it, you find compressed phrasing and surprising line breaks that force you to slow down and notice each word.

Dr. Seuss leans into rhyme, rhythm, and invented words. His sentences bounce. His vocabulary is playful. The structure of his language invites children to participate in the sound—and the whimsy—of it.

Sir Arthur Conan Doyle writes with a methodical, almost clinical precision. Through Watson's narration, even emotional events are filtered through observation and reason. The tone stays measured, events are linear. He guides you through the logic.

Tolkien, on the other hand, immerses you in layered description, deep history, invented languages, and a sense of mythic weight. He lingers. He builds. He wants you to feel the world as much as see it.

These authors are writing different kinds of stories, sure. But genre alone doesn't explain the difference. The distinction lies in their repeated narrative choices—what they emphasize, how they structure sentences, what emotional distance they maintain, and how much detail they allow on the page.

Voice lives in those decisions.

It is not just what you say. It's how you consistently choose to say it.

You can see this in nonfiction as well. Let's look at two history books covering the same topic—Mussolini.

First up: *Story of the World,* a history textbook for young people by Susan Wise Bauer.

> Mussolini's followers joined together in an organization that he called *Fasci di Combattimento*, or the "Band of Fighters." The word *fasci*, or "band" actually referred to the *fasces*, the bundle of tightly joined-together sticks with an ax in the center that had been a symbol of the ancient Roman government. Mussolini believed that individuals should be bound together

so tightly that they formed a single united state, and that this state could never be broken apart.

Although he held the title of prime minister, Mussolini was actually a military dictator. He wanted to build a new Roman Empire by recapturing all the land around the Mediterranean Sea. He knew that Romulus, the legendary founder of Rome, was supposed to have taken a plow and plowed out the borders of his new city. So, imitating Romulus, Mussolini got on a tractor and drove around the borders of new cities he hoped to build on his "new Roman Empire."

If Italy had to go to war to build this new empire, Mussolini would declare war.

Story of the World, Volume 4: The Modern Age by Susan Wise Bauer (2005: Peace Hill Press), pages 264-266

Bauer writes for homeschooled students, so she explains events with clarity and age-appropriate detail. She walks the reader through context and background, occasionally pausing to clarify terms. Her tone is educational but steady, and she usually includes a fun fact, like the tractor story.

Now check out *Don't Know Much About History* by Kenneth Davis, which is aimed at adults brushing up on history:

> In 1925, Mussolini installed himself as head of a single-party state he called *fascismo*. The word came from *fasces*, a Latin word referring to a bundle of rods bound around an ax, which had been a Roman symbol of authority. While most of Europe disarmed, Mussolini rearmed Italy during the twenties. A failure at actual governing, Mussolini saw military adventurism as the means to keep the Italian people loyal, and Italy embarked on war in Africa and in support of General Francisco Franco's Spanish rebels.
>
> *Don't Know Much About History* by Kenneth Davis (1990: Avon Books), page 288

See how Davis summarizes more briskly, focusing on political implications, and assuming a higher level of background knowledge? The sentences are tighter, the commentary sharper, and you can hear how it changes the feel of the story.

Still, they're about the same historical figure. Same basic facts. Just a different delivery.

That delivery is voice.

What Voice Isn't

Now, let's talk about what doesn't make voice.

It's not a gimmick. Writing in all lowercase like Cummings is not automatically voice. Rhyming everything doesn't make you Dr. Seuss. Long descriptions won't make you Tolkien. Those are expressions of voice, not the source of it.

Voice also isn't your genre. You can write science fiction with a solemn, meditative tone or with irreverent humor. You can write romance with lyrical prose or brisk dialogue. Genre shapes expectations, but it doesn't erase individuality.

Voice isn't the same thing as character voice, either. Your characters should sound different from one another (and preferably from you). A teenager shouldn't speak like a retired professor unless that contrast is intentional. But even when you're writing in first person, something of you—the author—remains in the structure, pacing, and worldview behind the narration.

And voice certainly isn't a mood you turn on and off at random. If your opening chapters are light and witty, and halfway through you shift into dense, academic exposition without warning or justification, readers will feel the jolt. Consistency matters.

So What Is Author Voice?

It's the recognizable pattern that emerges from your repeated narrative instincts. It grows out of your vocabulary preferences, your sentence rhythms, your approach to description, your treatment of characters, your tolerance for ambiguity, your sense of humor—or lack of it. Over time, those tendencies form a narrative fingerprint.

That fingerprint doesn't trap you. It doesn't limit you to one tone or one genre. It simply means that when you write, you leave traces of yourself on the page.

To develop author voice, you need to understand those traces, so that you can encourage them and learn how they serve you, so that eventually, you know your voice—and so will your reader.

In the next section, we're going to move from definition to dissection. We'll put voice under a microscope by comparing how different authors handle the same kind of scene—and why the results feel so different. That will show us how voice operates inside a specific kind of scene and what, exactly, creates that sense of difference on the page.

But before we go there, take a moment to consider your own writing.

Reflection Questions

- If someone read a paragraph of your work with the names removed, what elements might still give you away?
- Do you tend to favor dialogue, description, or interior thought?
- Are your sentences usually compact and direct, or layered and unfolding?
- How would you describe your vocabulary? (Academic, elementary, sensory-heavy, imaginative)
- What emotional distance do you keep from your characters—close, clinical, amused, sympathetic?
- What do you lean toward—humor? Introspection? Rich sensory experiences? High action and punchy sentences?

Exercise

Choose a paragraph or page from something you've written. Underline or highlight:

- Repeated sentence patterns
- Preferred kinds of detail
- Any consistent tonal quality

Don't judge it. Just observe it. Recognition is the first step toward ownership.

CHAPTER TWO

Discovering Your Voice

At the end of the last chapter, you looked at your own writing and marked patterns. I hope you did it—if not, go back and do it. It's a crucial part of discovering your voice because discovery begins with awareness.

Most writers assume voice is something they will "find" one day, as if it's waiting fully formed behind a curtain. In reality, your voice is already there.

Nor is it something you have to create so much as recognize and coax. Voice lives in your habits, in the repeated choices you make without thinking, and in the narrative instincts that feel so natural you hardly notice them.

The Clue Is in Your Instincts

A few years ago, I had some cognitive testing done because I was concerned about memory issues. One of the tests required me to list as many words as possible beginning with the letter F. As I worked through the exercise, I noticed something interesting: I was instinctively reaching for large, complex words. Forget "for, far, from" (or forget), I was spitting out "foreign, formaldehyde, frontier..."

I wasn't trying to impress anyone, and I certainly wasn't thinking about style. That was simply the vocabulary my brain defaulted to.

That moment told me something about my writing. My natural language setting leans toward a little more elevated. It also explained why writing for middle grade requires more conscious adjustment from me. The tendency itself wasn't good or bad. It was information.

Discovery works like that. You pay attention to what you do automatically.

When you draft a scene, what comes first? Dialogue? Action? Internal reflection? Do you compress description without thinking, or do you linger because atmosphere genuinely fascinates you? When tension increases, do your sentences shorten on their own, or do they expand as you layer in emotion and context?

Your habits are clues. They reveal what feels natural to you.

Look at What You Emphasize

One of the simplest ways to discover your voice is to examine emphasis. Not what you *think* you should emphasize, but what you naturally do.

Take an ordinary scene from your writing. Where does your attention settle? What receives the most space? If you introduce a setting, do you focus on sensory detail or move quickly to character interaction? If conflict arises, do you spend more time inside the character's emotional reaction or on the mechanics of what's happening?

Don't evaluate whether those choices are right. You only need to notice them.

Voice often hides in emphasis. What you slow down for signals what matters to you. What you glide past suggests what you consider secondary. Over time, those patterns become part of your narrative identity.

Think about your writing—or about the voices you love to read—and ask what makes them feel distinct. The answer almost always lies in emphasis.

Notice Your Emotional Distance

Another reliable indicator of voice is emotional distance. Some writers position the reader very close to the character's inner experience, filtering events through immediate thought and feeling. Others maintain a slight observational distance, allowing behavior and dialogue to suggest emotion rather than spelling it out.

Neither approach is inherently superior, and to be honest, you'll probably have some variation. However, when you look at your work as a whole, you'll see that you have a general tendency toward a style.

When you look at your own work, how close are you to your characters? Do you sit inside their heads, or do you observe them? Do you allow commentary, or do you stay neutral? Does your tone lean toward amused, analytical, tender, restrained?

You don't need to label yourself; just note the patterns.

Discovery is not about deciding what your voice should be. It's about acknowledging what it already is.

Listen to Yourself

Reading your work aloud can make your voice more obvious. When you hear your sentences, rhythm becomes clearer. You may notice that your prose tends to unfold in long, layered structures or that it moves briskly and directly.

You may hear a conversational tone you hadn't consciously intended, or a seriousness that carries through even light scenes.

You can have someone else read to you or even use text-to-speech. That will bring out different things, though, especially text-to-speech, because the computer will not have your emotional insights. This is a great exercise, though, for hearing the cadence of your writing—sentence lengths, vocabulary, lyrical rhythm.

Your Influences Are Showing

Voices do not spring up out of nothing. They are shaped by what you absorb.

- The books you read.
- The movies you watch.
- The shows you quote without realizing it.
- The essays you underline.
- The conversations that stay with you long after they end.

All of that feeds your narrative instincts.

If you grew up reading fast-paced thrillers, forward momentum may feel natural to you. If you love expansive fantasy, layered description may feel comfortable. If satire delights you, humor may slip into your writing almost unconsciously. These influences don't make your voice derivative. They give it texture.

Your voice is not a copy of what you consume. It is a reflection of what resonated deeply enough to shape you.

Take a moment to think about the storytellers who feel like home. Not the ones you admire out of obligation, but the ones you return to. What draws you back? Is it clarity? Wit? Emotional depth? Precision? Restraint?

Now look at your own writing. Where do you see echoes? Where do you see a difference?

Your voice grows in conversation with the voices you love.

Recognition Before Refinement

At this stage, you are not trying to change anything. You are not trying to become more lyrical, more concise, or more marketable. You are simply identifying what already exists on the page.

Look across multiple pieces of your work if you can. Different moods. Different subjects. Different goals. What remains consistent? What feels unmistakably yours?

How do you recognize yourself in your own sentences?

That recognition is the foundation for everything that follows.

You can't own your voice until you recognize it. In the next chapter, we'll explore how those patterns reveal themselves when tension increases and the story accelerates.

Reflection Questions

- What elements consistently receive the most space in your writing?
- How emotionally close does your narration stay to your characters?
- Which storytellers have influenced you most, and what do you love about their voice?
- When you read your work aloud, what rhythms and tones repeat?

Exercise

Choose two short scenes from different pieces you've written. Without revising them, read them side by side and mark recurring patterns in emphasis, rhythm, and emotional distance. Then list three storytellers whose work has shaped you. Compare the two sets of observations. Where do you see influence? Where do you see individuality?

CHAPTER THREE

Voice Under Pressure

It's one thing to recognize your voice in a reflective paragraph. It's another to see it when something explodes.

Pressure has a way of revealing instinct.

When tension rises—whether it's physical danger, emotional confrontation, or a high-stakes decision—and you're deep into what's going on, and your fingers are flying across the keyboard… When editing is the last thing on your mind, and you're writing for sheer joy (or because the scene or section has you by the throat and you must get it down)… That's when your habits become most visible.

Pressure on the page—which is different from deadline pressure, though that can work, too—makes you revert to Default Mode. You don't think about polishing or worry about making an impression. It's sheer *git 'er done* energy.

That's where voice shows itself most clearly.

What Happens to Your Sentences?

Go back to a tense moment in your writing. If you can find one before you've edited, that's even better—just ignore the urge to correct the typos and observe.

Did your sentences shorten automatically? Did the rhythm tighten? Or did your prose expand because you wanted readers to feel every flicker of internal reaction? Did you slow down to describe what was happening physically, or did you cut description and move straight to consequence?

How you react will both be determined by your voice and reveal your voice. Let's look at an example.

Comparing Voices Under Pressure

Let's take a look at voice in fight scenes from three authors: Edgar Rice Burroughs, Larry Correia, and Colleen Drippé. The situation in each was similar. An enemy appears. There is danger. The protagonist responds.

First, let's look at a classic: Edgar Rice Burroughs' *Land of Terror*:

> ...and close behind him, in single file, followed the others. They were armed precisely as were the Ruvans—two spears and a stone knife—and they were of the same race of fine-looking blacks. Only in their war paint did they differ in appearance from the warriors of Ruva.
>
> Silently I fitted an arrow to my bow and waited until the entire file was well within the ambush. I bent the bow and took careful aim. This was savage warfare, warfare of the Stone Age. Of course, we lacked poison gas, and we couldn't drop bombs on women and children and hospitals; but in our own primitive way we could do fairly well, and so I released my arrow, and as it sank deep into the body of the last man in the file, I gave the signal for the Ruvan warriors to attack.

With savage war cries they rose and hurled their spears. The warriors, taken entirely by surprise, were thrown into confusion, to which I added by driving half a dozen more arrows into as many of them in rapid succession.

Land of Terror by Edgar Rice Burroughs (1971: Ace Books), page 147

Now, Larry Correia's *Monster Hunter Bloodlines*:

One of the demon hounds appeared in the truck's bed and immediately started climbing in through the back window, snapping at Sonya. She shrieked but grabbed it by the ear and forced its head away. The girl had to be incredibly strong to shove that beast around like that, but she couldn't maneuver Abomination into it.

"Bad dog!"

I leaned back and shot the dog right between the shoulder blades. It ruptured, spraying fire all over the truck. Thankfully, the blue fire burned cold rather than hot, because that would have been awkward. This way we'd just have frostbite instead of third-degree burns.

Monster Hunter Bloodlines by Larry Correia (2021: Baen) eBook

Finally, Colleen Drippé's *Vessel of Darkness*:

Then he was crouching in the doorway, fighting for his life. It was not for nothing Spear had spent his earliest years in Arengarem's Drayak quarter. He and his brothers had been involved in more than one brawl with young Haveks. It also helped that he was a Gelan.

He managed to project a false warning behind them. As one of them turned, Spear dove in under the other one's arm, slashing at the legs and tumbling out into the corridor. One attacker was down, cursing as he bled from a deep cut below the knee. Spear projected again—something behind! Turn! Guard yourself!

This time the breed hesitated and came after Spear instead. The other one rose to his feet, still bleeding as he circled to get on the other side. The king avoided another slash and glimpsed movement in the corridor behind his attackers. Then one of them slipped on his own blood, giving Spear a chance to grapple with him.

Vessel of Darkness by Colleen Drippé (2024: Proxima Centauri), page 216

The differences are radical.

Larry Correia's scene moves fast. The prose feels immediate and kinetic. You're in motion almost from the first line. What stands out most, though, isn't just the pacing—it's the humor embedded in the danger. Even as something violent happens, there's a wry aside. The tone doesn't collapse into grim seriousness. Instead, it balances threat with personality. The action propels forward, and the humor sharpens the impact rather than undercutting it.

Edgar Rice Burroughs handles the same kind of moment very differently. His language lingers more. He paints the attackers visually. He describes their appearance and their formation before releasing the action. The pacing stretches slightly because immersion matters. You're meant to see the scene, not just experience the impact. He weaves in narrative commentary, a reflective tone that frames the violence within a broader perspective. The fight feels part of a larger world and history.

Colleen Drippé's scene tightens in another way. The prose narrows to what the character does and perceives. The focus is less on broad visual description and more on immediate action and reaction. The sentences are controlled and functional, and the tension builds through efficiency. You're not invited to linger. You're pulled through.

Same basic setup. Three distinct experiences.

None of these writers announces, "Here's my voice." It reveals itself through pacing, through what receives descriptive weight, through how much commentary is allowed on the page, and through tone under stress.

Voice under pressure isn't about what happens. It's about what the writer chooses to highlight.

Go back over these scenes and ask yourself which scene resonates with you the most. What is the author doing in that scene, and why does it feel more natural? Now look at your own writing. Do you see any similarities?

Where Does Your Attention Go?

When something goes wrong for your protagonist, where does your narrative attention point first?

- Do you focus on movement—who lunges, who falls, who fires, who misses?
- Do you focus on sensation—heat, impact, sound, breath?
- Do you focus on thought—*What just happened? How do I fix this?*
- Do you focus on interaction—who says what in the middle of chaos?

You don't consciously plan this most of the time. You react. That reaction reveals your priorities.

Voice under pressure becomes easier to identify because everything extraneous falls away. You can't hide behind elaborate exposition in a fight scene. You have to choose what matters most in the moment.

And those choices are rarely accidental.

Before we move on, think about the last high-stakes scene you wrote. If someone read it aloud without telling you it was yours, would you recognize the pacing? The tone? The way tension is handled?

These are clues into your unique voice.

Pacing Does Not Negate Voice

Certain scenes can demand certain paces, and that can make you feel like you need to sacrifice your voice to adapt.

For example, straight action, whether a fight scene or a race, often calls for more immediacy, quicker sentences, and snap decisions. It's tempting to think you need to set aside your voice to meet those needs. After all, the plot is speeding up, you've got to concentrate on the actual events, the physical stuff like ninja kicks or phaser fire. Tone gets lost in the immediacy of the action, right?

We've seen above that that's not so.

Others may fall into the trap that emotional tension needs to be handled in a specific way, perhaps the gazing unseeing out the window as the rain spatters the window and clouds coat the world in gray. Doesn't sadness have to be heavy and well, *sad*?

While there are certain expectations for high-tension scenes, that doesn't mean there's no room for your particular approach.

If you naturally lean toward humor, it may surface even when things are moving fast. It might not be slapstick—although that can happen (and does in my writing)—but perhaps a snarky one-liner or wry observation. If you tend toward restraint, your tense scenes may feel controlled rather than chaotic. If emotional intensity drives your storytelling, pressure may deepen internal experience instead of accelerating physical action.

Even the conventions of sentence structure can be violated when the voice is confident enough to carry the scene. High action and tension scenes usually mean shorter sentences, but Burrough's last sentence in the example above is 59 words long!

Now that doesn't mean you should ignore the conventions of writing just to indulge your voice. They're there for reasons rooted in our psyche.

That doesn't mean, however, that voice vanishes when the stakes rise. It adapts to them.

Look at one of your own high-stakes scenes and ask: Does this feel like the same writer who wrote my quieter moments? Or does it feel like I'm trying to imitate what I think action should sound like?

Instinct vs. Performance

Sometimes we *perform* tension. We pile on adjectives or adverbs—urgently, purposefully, yet...indulgently. We over-explain movement. We attempt to sound dramatic. The result is louder prose, not stronger prose.

However, when we relax into instinct, the writing becomes cleaner because we're focused on what matters to us (or our characters) in that moment.

The fight scene exercise works so well because it strips away distraction. When all you have is conflict on the page, you can't hide behind exposition or worldbuilding. Your rhythm, your emphasis, your tonal leanings become obvious.

Try this with your own work. Take a tense scene and read it aloud. Then ask yourself: Does this sound like me? Or does it sound like the version of me trying to impress someone?

Under pressure, authenticity becomes visible.

But I Write Nonfiction!

Even nonfiction has its moments of pressure, and though they might not be action scenes, they can still demonstrate how your voice comes out in earnestness or tension.

Pressure in nonfiction often looks different. It isn't a sword fight or a demon hound climbing into a truck. It's a difficult historical truth. A controversial claim. A deeply personal confession. A moral challenge to the reader. Those moments carry weight, and how you handle that weight reveals your voice just as clearly as any battle scene.

Consider historians writing about a brutal event. One might describe the event in restrained, factual language, allowing the horror to emerge through documented detail alone. Another might reflect on the human cost, guiding the reader to empathy over academic knowledge. A third might frame the event within a broader pattern of political failure, emphasizing systemic causes rather than individual suffering.

They are writing about the same event, but their voice is clear in how they handle it.

Or think about memoir. When you reach a painful personal memory, you have choices. You might narrate the scene with quiet understatement, trusting readers to feel the weight without overt commentary. You might walk them through your internal thoughts in real time, exposing vulnerability. Or you might opt for reflective distance, analyzing your younger self with insight and compassion. Or you could make a joke of it. Each approach creates a different experience of tension.

Devotional and inspirational nonfiction have their own pressure points. When you challenge readers to examine their beliefs or behavior, your tone matters. One writer may adopt a gentle, companionable voice: *Let's think about this together*. Another may speak with direct conviction, pressing for change with urgency. A third may lean heavily into storytelling first, allowing the lesson to emerge gradually. The core message might be similar. The delivery is not.

Nonfiction pressure often shows up in moments of earnestness. When you care deeply about what you're saying, your voice becomes more visible. Do you intensify your language? Do you simplify it? Do you step closer to the reader, or do you maintain analytical distance?

Look at one of your own nonfiction passages where something important is at stake. Perhaps you're explaining a painful social reality, sharing a personal turning point, or arguing for a principle you believe in strongly. Read that section aloud. Notice what changes. Does your pacing slow? Do your sentences grow more deliberate? Does your tone become firmer or more reflective?

Just as in fiction, pressure strips away the optional. What remains is what matters most to you.

And that is where voice lives.

Examples of Nonfiction Voice Under Pressure

I read a lot of time management books. You'd think one would be enough—how much can you say about managing your time? Surprisingly, everyone has a different angle: Matthew Kelly in *Slowing Down to the Speed of Joy* takes a spiritual approach; Carl Newport homes in on focus in *Deep Work*; meanwhile, Nir Eyal in *Indistractable* goes straight toward managing distractions. It's more than approach, though. Their voices are night and day.

Compare Newport and Kelly when dealing with the concept of busyness.

> **Busyness as a Proxy for Productivity:** In the absence of clear indicators of what it means to be productive and valuable in their jobs, many knowledge workers turn back to an industrial indicator of productivity: doing lots of stuff in a visible manner.

> *Deep Work* by Carl Newport (2016: Grand Central Publishing), page 64

This is a topic that hits home—busyness is not just a flex; it's about job security and proving you have value. Yet Newport tells you this in a calm, academic way.

Now look at Kelly's approach:

> Ten years ago, a friend asked me a question that was so rudimentary, and yes, I had never even considered it: "Do you think you are doing enough?"
>
> The question was bewildering. I didn't even know how to consider the question at first. The concept of doing enough was so foreign. But the question burrowed deep in my heart and began to go to work. And at times when my schedule reached obvious layers of insanity, the question would announce itself again: "Do you feel like you are doing enough?"
>
> *Slowing Down to the Speed of Joy* by Matthew Kelly (2024: Blue Sparrow), page 2

See how much more personally Kelly approaches the problem?

But also look at the vocabulary: "Productive and valuable in their jobs" vs "are you doing enough?" "Absence of clear indicators" vs "a question so bewildering." One engages the intellect; the other, the heart.

Both are valid in approach and in acknowledging the importance of the topic. The difference is in the voice.

What Pressure Reveals

In calmer scenes, you may consciously craft your prose, but in tense scenes, you reveal your reflexes. So, pressure in a story shows what you instinctively value. It exposes patterns, clarifies pacing, highlights emotional distance.

That isn't something to fix, even if it seems to violate convention. It's something to observe and explore.

Watch what your writing does when the stakes rise. That's where your narrative fingerprint often sharpens into focus.

In the next chapter, we'll slow down and examine the individual components that create those patterns—so you can see exactly how they work together on the page.

Reflection Questions

- When tension increases, what happens to your sentence length and rhythm?
- In high-stakes scenes, do you emphasize action, emotion, or dialogue first?
- Does your tone remain consistent under pressure?
- Does your tense writing feel natural—or artificially heightened for effect?

Exercise

Choose a fight, confrontation, or emotionally charged scene from your own work. Read it aloud and mark shifts in pacing, emphasis, and tone compared to a calmer scene. Then rewrite a single paragraph from that scene, exaggerating your natural tendency—lean further into speed, or internal thought, or humor. Notice how quickly your voice becomes more pronounced.

CHAPTER FOUR

Building Your Voice Without Becoming a Clone

Once you've recognized your patterns, the next step is to strengthen them intentionally.

There are ways to do that. When you edit, you can search for places where you can make things sound "more you." You can ask beta readers to let you know where things "slow down" or where they skim paragraphs. This isn't always a matter of plot or pacing but where your distinctive expression has gotten lazy or generic.

But all that is awareness and tweaking. What about training? The best way to learn is by studying others.

Sometimes, an author sees someone else's style and tries to imitate it. This is great when doing a pastiche (check out Ann Margaret Lewis' *The Watson Chronicles*), but you should have an eye for developing your own voice, and that happens best when it grows out of who you already are, not when you try to graft someone else's style onto your work.

That said, you absolutely can train voice by incorporating aspects that you admire in other authors that you like. Remember what I'd said above about influences? The trick is to go beyond their style to make it your own.

Let's dig into that now.

Mimicry as Muscle Training

When I say mimicry, I don't mean plagiarism, and I don't mean a carbon copy (unless you are purposely doing a pastiche or a straight-up parody). I mean study.

If there's an author whose work you admire, don't just read them casually. Read them with attention. Notice how the clauses fit together. Feel the pacing. Outline the rise and fall of action and emotion to really grasp the story beats.

This isn't about becoming that author. It's about strengthening your awareness. When you understand how something is built, you gain more control over how you build.

Actors do this constantly. Comedians do it too. They study timing. They absorb rhythm. They try on different deliveries until they understand what makes something land.

Writers can do the same. Mimicking, done intentionally, is training. It stretches your range without replacing your identity.

Studying Tone Without Becoming a Clone

I'm a fun writer and proud of it. My favorite reviews are when someone compares me to Terry Pratchett or Douglas Adams.

Nonetheless, there was a year when I felt like my writing was getting stale, so I asked my husband (the perfect writer's spouse) to give me a challenge. He said, "Put *The Old Man and the Sea* in space." It was a terrific idea, not just for the thematic elements but because Hemingway's voice is so different from mine.

I wanted *The Old Man and the Void* to carry an echo of Hemingway, so I had to understand his voice. I didn't sit down and try to imitate him line by line. Instead, I read the book, taking copious notes of what he did and why. Then I went online to find other analyses of his style. I wanted to understand what people consistently identified as distinctive about his writing. What created that tone? What gave it that particular feel?

Once I understood the broader characteristics—restraint, structure, pacing—I could experiment thoughtfully inside my own story. The result wasn't Hemingway by a long shot—but it also was something unlike what I'd ever written before: If I could describe it, *The Old Man and the Void* had a masculine strength. It was still me, but my study of Hemingway added a nuance I didn't know I had—and that's stayed with me in subsequent books.

That's the difference between borrowing technique and borrowing identity.

If there's a part of your voice you want to strengthen, or if there's a "void" in your style you think needs exploring, I highly recommend a deep study and re-imagining of someone else's work.

Write It Out by Hand

This sounds old-fashioned, but it works.

If there's a passage you admire for tone, copy it out by hand. Don't skim it. Don't type it. Write it. Your brain processes structure differently when your hand moves through the sentence.

You begin to notice cadence. Where clauses sit. How verbs carry weight. How description is layered—or withheld.

This is a great exercise if you have problem areas in your writing, too. You're building technical awareness so you can exercise more technical control in your own work.

Analyze Before You Imitate

One mistake writers make is trying to sound like someone without understanding why that writer sounds that way.

Instead of asking, "How do I sound like Tolkien?" ask, "What specifically does Tolkien emphasize?" (We'll look at detailed examples later.) Is it depth of history? Layered description? Formal diction? Mythic tone?

When you break voice into components, it becomes trainable.

I've heard that you can experiment with AI for comparison by taking a paragraph you've written and asking it to rewrite the paragraph in the style of a particular author. Then you compare versions: What changed? Sentence length? Vocabulary? Emotional distance?

Personally, I'd be cautious. I once stuck my work into an AI evaluator to see what author I wrote like. I used the same page of text, but depending on the amount of prose I put in for evaluation, it gave me wildly different answers. Make your own judgement

Used carefully, comparison sharpens awareness.

Get Feedback on Voice—Not Just Grammar

When you seek feedback, make sure you're asking the right questions.

If you only ask whether something is clear or technically correct, you'll receive line edits. Those matter—but they won't help you understand voice.

Instead, ask readers what stands out about the way you tell the story. Ask questions like:

- Does my narration feel distinct?
- Are there places where the tone shifts unexpectedly?
- What storytelling strengths are most obvious?
- Are there places where your attention wanders even when the tension is high?

The goal isn't to chase praise. It's to identify patterns.

Sometimes other people see your voice more clearly than you do.

If you don't have beta readers who can do this for you, you can try AI. I have put my own work into AI and asked it to uncover my strengths and weaknesses, and it gave me what I would consider a reasonably accurate description—although it can lean toward complimentary. (AI is such a sycophant!)

Write Across Range

Another way to strengthen your voice is to place it in different environments, like I did when applying my love of sci-fi to re-imagining *The Old Man and the Sea*.

It doesn't have to be a whole book, of course. Write something lighter than your usual tone. Try something darker. Write a scene with almost no dialogue. Write one built almost entirely from dialogue. Write in first person if you usually prefer third.

You'll discover two things. First, certain elements of your voice remain steady. Second, some elements stretch more easily than others.

That information is valuable. It tells you what's foundational and what's flexible. It may also identify weaknesses you want to work on.

Write. Then Write More.

The most reliable way to strengthen your voice is still the simplest: write, and keep writing.

You've probably heard the saying that it takes a million words to become a writer. Whether the number is accurate is less important than the principle. Repetition clarifies identity.

The more you write, the more your patterns stabilize. What once felt accidental begins to feel intentional as your defaults become your strengths.

The key is to let your words flow naturally in the draft and remain aware of your strengths and unique voice while editing. Use your writing skill to support your voice, just as your voice enhances your skill.

Building your voice isn't about becoming someone else. It's about strengthening the parts of your writing that are already yours.

In the next chapter, we'll talk about what can quietly undermine that process—and how to avoid it without losing your confidence on the page.

Reflection Questions

- Which authors influence you most, and what techniques—not characters—do you admire in their writing?
- When you experiment with a different style, what feels natural and what feels forced?
- What feedback have you received that points to recurring strengths in your writing?

Exercise

Choose a short paragraph from your work. Rewrite it in three different ways:

- With tighter, leaner sentences
- With expanded description
- With more internal reflection

Then compare all versions to your original. Which elements remain consistent? Which shifts feel authentic? Which feel artificial?

CHAPTER FIVE

What Gets in the Way

Once you begin to recognize and build your voice, a new challenge appears.

You can accidentally sand it down in the editing process or dilute it by adding elements that aren't you but that you think "should" be there.

Most voice problems don't come from lack of talent. They come from interference.

Overediting Yourself Into Oblivion

Sloppiness isn't voice. You need to edit your work, but there's a difference between refining and flattening.

Sometimes writers revise with the unconscious goal of sounding "correct." They remove unusual phrasing. They smooth sentence rhythm until everything feels uniform. They cut anything that might be considered distinctive because they're afraid it sounds awkward.

The result is technically clean and emotionally neutral.

In fiction, this often shows up when dialogue loses its personality. Every character begins to speak in the same balanced, tidy sentences. Granted, fictional dialogue needs to be cleaner and make more sense than the average conversation overheard in the coffee shop, but there is room for personality even in the simplest sentence.

In nonfiction, it can happen when strong opinions are softened so thoroughly that the writing feels vague. If you find yourself deleting every sentence that feels bold or slightly risky, pause before you hit backspace. Ask whether the sentence is unnecessary—or merely personal. Those are not the same thing.

AI editors like Grammarly or Spellcheck can also remove your voice in the name of "clarity" or even "sensitivity" or what we used to call "political correctness." (I think Word now includes that under "Vocabulary.") Have confidence—if you wrote a word or phrase for a reason and it's clear (and not going to get you investigated by the FBI), don't change it just because Grammarly has underlined it in yellow.

Trying to Sound Impressive

I have a T-shirt of Yoda at a typewriter. It says, "Metaphors be with you." It's too tight, which is kind of a metaphor in itself, because I'm not comfortable with metaphors in my writing.

However, it does illustrate another issue that can get in the way of your voice: the need to *perform*. You know, delving into the thesaurus for grander words, indulging in elaborate metaphors, or opting for heavier phrasing in order to sound profound.

Sometimes, we do it to show off. Sometimes, we feel like it's expected. But unless you're writing for a school assignment, you're not doing yourself, your story, or your reader any favors.

Now, don't get me wrong. If elevated language is your natural default, that's one thing. Also, certain genres may call for certain language conventions. Literary, for example, thrives on deep metaphor, and academic books are going to be heavier on terminology and explanatory style. However, if you only use it when you're trying to sound important, readers will feel the strain—your strain as well as theirs.

For example, your reader may stop connecting to your heartfelt personal essay if you decide to veer into flowery metaphor or "socially conscious" commentary on a somewhat applicable but tangential issue. In the meantime, humor in the wrong place can throw a reader out of the tension of the scene.

Even within genres, there's room for voice. The time management examples clearly show that. There's a whole realm of Regency Romance where the heroine is a spunky, independent feminist more suited for the 1960s and everyone around her just goes with it.

Personally, that drives me nuts, but other readers love it, which makes it a good example of audience expectations as much as author choice. But if you do it inauthentically, readers will pick up on it.

Your voice is strongest when it sounds like you, not like the version of you trying to impress a panel of judges.

Naturally, I'm not saying not to stretch your talent or twist a genre or experiment. Like we discussed in the chapter above, those help you grow as a writer. Just do it in service to the story and your reader, not because you think your voice doesn't measure up.

Trend-Chasing

Every few years, certain styles dominate. Minimalism becomes fashionable. Then lush prose returns. Then clipped, cinematic pacing takes over. Social media favors punchy lines and quotable fragments.

It's easy to absorb those trends and assume that's what your writing should look like, or even fear that unless you change your writing, you'll be unpublishable.

There's nothing wrong with learning from current styles. The problem comes when you override your instincts to match them.

If your natural pacing is reflective and layered, forcing yourself into ultra-minimalist prose may leave you sounding thin. If your natural tone includes humor, stripping it away because "serious books don't do that" may flatten your work.

Your voice can evolve and even adapt. For example, the first paragraph in this section follows a more market, blog-like trend that really isn't my usual style, but I think it works here.

You can adjust your style. Just don't let it disappear.

Besides, the trends will change, or (even better) by bucking the trend, you become a fresh voice that sets the next Great Style. Plus, regardless of current conventions, great prose endures. *The Lord of the Rings* and *The Chronicles of Narnia* came out in the same era and are radically different in their author voices, yet both have stood the test of time.

There is room for your writing style.

Comparison

Comparison is one of the fastest ways to undermine confidence in any endeavor, but especially in writing.

You read an author whose prose feels effortless, and suddenly your own sentences feel clumsy or shallow. So you revise not because something is wrong, but because you no longer trust your instincts.

You read someone's book in your research, and start to doubt whether your perspective isn't authoritative enough. Or maybe their approach is so different from yours, and you wonder if you're coming on too strong. So, you hedge. You soften. You dilute high-impact but blunt statements with excessive qualifiers and what you hope is a more "understanding" tone.

Comparison is inevitable. To be a good writer, you need to be a good reader. You need to absorb books, consider styles, and sometimes even strive toward them. Growth requires study and work and finding the next objective to aspire to, such as someone else's dialogue skill.

It does not, however, require self-erasure.

When comparison pushes you toward improvement, it's useful. When it pushes you toward silence, it's destructive.

Fear of Being "Too Much"

Some writers worry they are too funny. Too intense. Too sentimental. Too analytical. Too blunt. Too—pick a feature!

So they tone themselves down.

This can be especially tempting in nonfiction like memoir and devotional writing. You may hesitate to express strong emotion or conviction because you don't want to alienate readers.

It happens in fiction, too. You may soften a character's sharp edges because you're afraid they'll be unlikable, or you may worry that your focus—whether on guns and violence or a Pro-Life worldview—will alienate your readers.

But voice lives in those edges.

That doesn't mean you ignore craft or audience. It also doesn't mean there aren't limits to what you do. More than once in my humorous stories, my husband or my crit group will tell me I crossed the line in a joke so that it no longer serves the story or character.

However, you need to consider why you're trimming. Do it with purpose and precision, not insecurity or the feeling that "they" won't approve.

Readers connect to specificity and passion, not neutrality.

Too Many Voices in the Room

Feedback is invaluable. It can also become overwhelming.

If five beta readers each suggest slightly different tonal adjustments, you can end up trying to satisfy all of them. The manuscript becomes a compromise of competing preferences.

You are not obligated to adopt every recommendation. Instead of asking, "How do I fix this?" try asking, "Which of these suggestions aligns with my voice and my goals?"

Alternatively, if several critiquers have an issue with a section, ask yourself why you're not communicating your point there. It could be a craft rather than a voice issue.

Discernment protects voice.

Artificial Intelligence and Other Cybernetic "Helpers"

AI has wormed itself into every aspect of business, from Spellcheck finding your typos to Jasper writing that email to your boss. A lot of writers fear it. Others have jumped on the bandwagon to mass-produce books and articles.

For discerning readers, the difference between AI-written and human-written work is identifiable, and it's not because of em-dashes. (Personally, I love a good em-dash, and no one has accused me of being an AI.)

Does that mean we should avoid AI at all costs? No. For one thing, you can't. It's just everywhere. If you run Spellcheck, you are using AI.

Why does AI wreck voice? Because of how it has learned. It scans the whole internet for language and phrases and puts them into an algorithm. Have you ever typed something into Google Search and seen how it tries to predict the next word? This is a more sophisticated version of the same thing.

What that means is *your* next word might not be the next word of the majority of the internet—especially when the majority of the internet is comprised of websites, business writing, and people's blogs about how they make $10,000 a month using AI to write books—*and now you can, too!*

What it does mean is that we have to use it well while guarding our voice. Typos and misspellings aside, any fiction writer worth their words knows not to trust Grammarly's helpful advice when "correcting" dialogue. Microsoft is even worse for understanding context and author voice. Just yesterday, it wanted to change

"I tried this" to "I'm tired of this"...although maybe that was a commentary on the manuscript?

AI has its uses, even beyond spellcheck.

My Not-So-Secret Secret

I'm going to let you in on a not-so-secret secret and hope you don't hate me for it: This book was written with the help of ChatGPT. It did not, however, write the book. Rather, I fed it the classes I taught, the notes I've taken, and a style guide, then told it to craft an outline. It came up with a draft.

In the draft phase, I gave it revision direction after revision direction, often repeating myself because it would fall back into its generic "Internet Everyman" voice. Then I went through the finished draft with a fine-toothed comb, adding, revising, rewriting just about everything, and building it into the book in your hands.

If you read my fiction, you'll see that the voice here is different. There may be some residual AI influence, but my approach has changed to meet genre expectations and the purpose of a book that teaches writing. I'd say the voice in this book is a nice compromise between my fiction and my business writing I do for corporations.

I would not recommend new writers use AI. I have 30 years of writing experience in fiction and nonfiction. I know my voice and I know how to fight a machine for it. *Not today, Skynet!*

Bonus for me, though: There are a lot fewer typos for Spellcheck to flag.

Voice rarely disappears dramatically. It fades through small, cautious decisions. It's like death from a thousand papercuts—something many of us pre-computer authors can relate to! Now you know some of the most insidious ways your voice can be muffled. Protect yourself!

Your voice makes an impression. In the next chapter, we'll talk about how that reveals itself from the very first page of your manuscript.

Reflection Questions

- Where might you be editing out something that actually sounds like you?
- Do you tend to overedit until your writing feels neutral?
- When you revise, are you clarifying—or performing?
- Have you softened strong passages out of fear of reader reaction?
- Do you try to satisfy every critique at once?

Exercise

Take a recent passage you've revised heavily. Compare the earliest draft to the latest version. Highlight differences in tone, sentence rhythm, and emphasis. Ask yourself whether the revisions strengthened clarity or muted personality.

CHAPTER SIX

Page One

There's a simple rule I'd heard from editor Michelle Buckman that has stayed with me over the years: *Your voice should be evident from page one.*

Not your plot twist. Not your backstory. Not your entire thematic arc.

Your voice.

Books are a commitment. Readers decide quickly whether you are worth their time. They may not consciously analyze sentence rhythm or tonal consistency, but they feel it. Within a paragraph or two, they know whether their time will be rewarded. Your voice as much as your words will tell them if they are in for a tear-jerker or spit-out-your-soda humor. They'll know whether and to what degree the book will inform, educate, or inspire.

Voice is felt immediately because it governs everything else, and when your voice is confident, it inspires confidence in the reader. That's true whether you're writing with authority or in vulnerability.

Why Voice Is Felt Immediately

On the first page of a novel, readers are listening for rhythm and tone. Are the sentences lean or layered? Is the narrative close to the character or slightly distant? Does humor surface? Is the prose restrained, lyrical, blunt?

Consider how differently a story might begin.

> On one otherwise normal Tuesday evening, I had the chance to live the American dream. I was able to throw my incompetent jackass of a boss from a fourteen-story window.
>
> *Monster Hunters International* by Larry Correia (2009: Baen), page 1

Immediately, you know this is going to be a wild no-holds-barred ride. You can expect some violence—but also some sardonic humor.

Now compare it to this:

> "There are dragons in the twins' vegetable garden."
>
> Meg Murry took her head out of the refrigerator where she had been foraging for an after-school snack and looked at her brother. "What?"
>
> "There are dragons in the twins' vegetable garden. Or there were. They've moved to the north pasture now."
>
> *A Wind in the Door* by Madeleine L'Engle (1973: Dell Publishing), page 1

There's still the promise of adventure, but we know things will be gentler.

One more:

> Ydrel threw himself into wakefulness with such force that he sat up in bed. Still, the nightmare images clung to his mind: the beat of a hundred hearts, the smell of sweat and fear. He clutched his stomach and fought the urge to scream.

A hundred bodies crowded around him, crushing him against the splintered wood of the boxcar.

No, this isn't real!

No room to move. No air to breathe. Suffocating. Drowning.

No, this isn't me!

Confusion and fear. Fear the trip would never end. Terror of what waited at its completion.

No! These aren't my memories!

Madness Bound by Karina Fabian (2025: Laser Cow Press), page 1

Immediately, you know there's going to be conflict, a lot of mental anguish and confusion, and probably not much humor.

In nonfiction, the effect is just as immediate.

It was the darkest day of my life.

I sat in a cell in London's Wormwood Scrubs prison on the second day of a twelve month prison sentence.

It was not the first time I'd been to prison...

> *Race with the Devil* by Joseph Pearce (2013: St. Benedict Press), page 1

Immediately, you are put into the POC of Joseph. You know this is biographical, urgent, and tense.

Compare it to:

> Imagine for a moment that you are the manager of a day-care center. You have a clearly stated policy that children are supposed to be picked up by 4 p.m. But very often parents are late. The result: at day's end, you have some anxious children and at least one teacher who must wait around for the parents to arrive. What to do?
>
> A pair of economists who heard of this dilemma—it turned out to be a rather common one—offered a solution: fine the tardy parents. Why, after all, should the day care center take care of these kids for free?
>
> *Freakonomics* by Steven D. Levitt and Stephen J. Dubner (2006: William Morrow), page 1

This one, by title and opening, tells you we'll be discussing economic issues, but in a concrete rather than merely academic way.

One more, also instructional and friendly, but note the different tone.

> A well-known scientist (some say it was Bertrand Russell) once gave a public lecture on astronomy. He described how the earth orbits around the sun and how the sun, in turn, orbits around the center of a vast collection of stars called our galaxy. At the end of the lecture, a little old lady at the back of the room got up and said: "What you have told us is rubbish. The world is really a flat disk supported on the back of a giant tortoise." The scientist gave a superior smirk before replying, "What is the tortoise standing on?" "You're very clever, young man, very clever," said the old lady, "But it's turtles all the way down!"
>
> Most people would find the picture of our universe as an infinite tower of tortoises rather ridiculous, but why do we think we know better? What do we know about the universe and how do we know it?

A Brief History of Time by Stephen W. Hawking (1988: Bantam Books), page 1

The cadence, the long first paragraph, the questions in the second paragraph...Despite starting with a joke, you get the feeling that you're in for something academic and thoughtful.

Every one of these examples has a unique voice, yet they have one thing in common: You can sense it from the opening paragraphs, and it tells you (without telling you) what you can expect. That's what makes a reader buy your book or search Amazon for the next one on the list.

Before readers commit to content, they commit to voice.

If the first page feels generic, cautious, or overly polished, they sense it. (Another reason readers can tell AI vs. real authors.) If it feels authentic, they want more.

Voice can tell a reader what to expect faster than exposition ever could.

Testing Voice on the First Page

One of the easiest ways to test your voice is simply to read it aloud, naturally, not dramatically. Do you hear rhythm? Does it feel like your narrative personality? Or does it sound like you're trying to write what you think an opening "should" sound like?

Here's another idea: Hand your first paragraphs to someone and ask what they expect from the rest of the piece. If they say, "It feels clear and practical," or "I expect a lot of reflection," or "Omigosh, this'll be hilarious," your voice is already signaling direction. If they struggle to describe it, you may still be warming up on the page.

First pages should not feel like throat-clearing.

They should feel intentional.

The Breakfast Eggs Exercise

Sometimes, writers, especially fiction writers, think that grabbing someone on Page One means starting with big drama, high tension, urgent stakes. But that's not true. With authentic voice, you can grab your reader with the most mundane things.

Like eggs.

When I teach voice in webinar, and I want to show how everyone has a voice, I ask my attendees to describe someone making eggs.

That's it. No dragons. No trauma. No dramatic business pivot. Just eggs.

Why eggs? Because the situation removes plot from the equation. Without high stakes, your voice has nowhere to hide. You can't rely on tension or spectacle. What remains is how you naturally tell a moment.

Here are three brief versions of the same neutral action.

> "I cracked the egg too hard and watched a shard of shell dive into the bowl like it had a death wish. Typical. Even breakfast required search and rescue."

That voice leans humorous and self-aware.

> "The egg split cleanly. The yolk held its shape, gold and unbroken, as it slid into the waiting pan."

This one is restrained and sensory-focused.

> "I whisked the eggs mechanically, trying not to think about Roy's many texts waiting unanswered on my phone."

Here, the action becomes emotional framing. The eggs are a backdrop for internal tension.

The action is identical. The voice is not.

You can expand the exercise further to see how your voice carried over genres. Write the egg scene as the opening of a thriller, where the crack of the shell foreshadows danger. Write it as a devotional reflection about daily bread. Write it as a business blog post about morning routines and productivity.

Regardless of genre or purpose, a strong opening will draw your reader, and that starts with a strong voice.

Fiction and Nonfiction on Page One

In fiction, voice on page one often shows up in how quickly you anchor us in character. Do we enter through action, thought, dialogue, or setting? Even minimal openings carry tone. A sparse first paragraph signals restraint. A sensory-rich opening signals immersion.

In nonfiction, page one must do two things at once: establish authority and establish tone.

Consider two openings for books on (one of my favorite topics) *Star Trek*:

> *Star Trek* is an unparalleled phenomenon that has fascinated, challenged, inspired, and of course entertained us for nearly 35 years. With a view of the future that began with the voyages of the original *Enterprise, Star Trek* imagines a universe of advanced technology, adventure on a galactic scale, and unabridged optimism for humanity's ethical progress.
>
> *The Ethics of Star Trek* by Judith Barad, Ph.D. (2000: Harper Collins), page 1

And now, this one:

> Every Star Trek fan has a favorite series. For many older fans in particular, *The Original Series* (1966-1969)—which used its iconic characters to hold up an allegorical mirror to one of the most tumultuous and influential areas of modern U.S. history while virtually inventing fan culture as we know it—remains unsurpassable. Others prefer the franchise's most commercially and critically successful outing, *The Next Generation* (1987-94), whose remarkable ensemble cast and winning blend of workplace drama and detective procedural turned the cerebral exploration of post-scarcity utopia into must-see TV while essentially creating the market (and as we will see, the business model) for space opera.
>
> *Late Star Trek: The Final Frontier in the Franchise Era* by Adam Kotsko (2025: University of Minnesota Press), page 1

Both establish authority with facts and language while also giving the impression that the authors don't just know the series, but respect it. They both set expectations immediately.

In all cases, readers are asking a quiet question: *Do I want to spend time with this voice?*

That question is answered before the plot unfolds.

A Practical First-Page Checklist

Before you move on from your opening, consider:

- Does this sound like me, or like my idea of what an opening should sound like?
- Is the tone consistent with the rest of the manuscript?
- Am I being clear, or am I hedging?
- Have I edited for clarity without flattening personality?
- Does the rhythm feel intentional?

You are not trying to impress, although you will if you do well enough. More importantly, though, you are trying to generate expectations that will make your reader turn the page.

Page one is not about fireworks. It's about confidence.

Your first page doesn't need to announce everything about your book. But it should set the stage and generate expectations that make the reader want to turn the page.

In the next chapter, we'll explore how genre shapes voice without confining it—both in fiction and in nonfiction.

Reflection Questions

- When you think about your favorite books, what do you remember about their opening pages—plot details, or the feeling of the voice?
- If someone read only your first page, what expectations would they form about the rest of the book? Would those expectations be accurate?
- If someone unfamiliar with your work read only your opening paragraph, what might they assume about you as a writer? Would that assumption match how you see yourself?
- When you revise your first page, are you focused primarily on information—or on establishing expectations through voice?

Exercise

Take your current first paragraph and rewrite it three different ways:

1. Lean into your natural tendency. If you're concise, make it cleaner. If you're reflective, allow more interior thought.
2. Exaggerate the opposite of your instinct. If you usually write lean, make it expansive. If you tend to layer reflection, make it brisk and action-oriented.
3. Return to your original tone, but refine it with full awareness of your voice.

Compare the three versions. Which one feels most authentic? Which one feels like performance?

CHAPTER SEVEN

Voice and Genre

Switching genres is fun. It's a good way to exercise creativity and stretch your skills, but there can be an unspoken assumption that genre dictates voice, and if you move from fantasy to romance, from memoir to business writing, or from devotional to secular nonfiction, you'll have to reinvent yourself entirely.

It's true that you may need to adjust your approach. Each genre has its own set of expectations. Nonetheless, the "you" does not disappear simply because the container changes.

I've written irreverently funny novels. I've written reverently Catholic novels. I've written secular family drama with deep emotional weight. I've also written product reviews, business articles, and artist features for online and local magazines.

On the surface, those categories look unrelated. It's true that they are different types of writing. The tone shifts. They have different audiences with different expectations. A novel gives me room for dialogue and character arcs. A business article demands clarity and concision. A product review requires objective evaluation and specificity.

Yet when I look across all of them, certain elements remain consistent.

I write in a practical, to-the-point way rather than a flowery one, but I tend toward conversational rather than academic, which can mean fun tangents now and again. My humor finds a way into the plot, even in serious topics, though it adjusts to the context. I emphasize the concrete. In fiction, that often means dialogue and action over long scenic description. In business writing, it means focusing on specific issues and actionable advice instead of abstract theory. I'm a minimalist when it comes to scenery, but when I do describe something, it's with purpose.

The genre shifts. The voice adapts. The core remains.

That's the distinction that matters. So let's talk about how your voice can adapt as you move through different genres. By the way, "genre" is being used to differentiate between types of nonfiction as well as fiction.

Genre Is a Container, Not a Costume

Genre sets expectations. Readers pick up a thriller expecting tension and forward motion. They open a memoir expecting personal reflection. They choose a self-help book expecting clarity and application. Those expectations are not arbitrary. They shape pacing, structure, and emphasis.

Even so, meeting expectations does not require wearing a different personality like a costume.

If you naturally lean toward concise prose, that quality can serve you in fiction and nonfiction alike. If humor is part of how you process the world, it may show up differently in a devotional than in a parody novel, but it doesn't have to vanish. If you prefer concrete examples over abstraction, that instinct strengthens business articles just as much as it sharpens storytelling.

Your voice is comprised of tools, and tools can be used for a variety of projects.

Fiction Across Categories

An irreverent space adventure and a more solemn, faith-infused story may differ in tone, but the same writer still chooses how long to linger on description, how much intelligence to grant characters, how tightly to pace dialogue. Even when the emotional register changes, patterns persist.

If you move from comedy to drama, you may dial humor back. You may deepen internal reflection. You may slow down the pacing in key moments. Those are adjustments of emphasis, not erasure of identity.

Readers who follow an author across series often do so because they recognize something consistent beneath the surface.

One of my favorite authors is Jane Lebak. She writes quirky fantasy with angels battling demons. She also writes cozy small-town romance under the pen name Maddie Evans.

Obviously, her *Seven Archangels* books won't sound exactly the same as *Operation Christmas Ring,* but when I read them, I can see the author behind the story. For example, she has a flair for sharing deep details about the most ordinary things. In fact, that's why I, who am not a romance reader, will read any book by Maddie Evans. I'm bound to learn something new and interesting. She brings that same love of factoids into her *Seven Archangels* books, usually through the Archangel Gabriel.

You can see it in how she handles romance and friendships as well: easy on the physicality with a stronger lean toward emotions and general lifting each other up. Even when the characters aren't religious, there's a spiritual underpinning in the worldview.

You'll notice that I've not said anything about word choice or sentence structure. I could probably find similarities if I went back and did the analysis, but in truth, that's not the part I think about when I think of her stories.

Nonfiction Across Categories

Nonfiction functions the same way.

A product review demands specificity and clarity. A business article calls for a structured argument and practical takeaways. An artist feature invites narrative framing and attention to personality. A memoir requires vulnerability and reflection.

Each category asks different things of you. But if you value practicality, you'll likely emphasize usable insight in all of them. If you gravitate toward concrete detail, you'll anchor abstract ideas in examples. If you favor lean prose, you'll resist unnecessary modifiers and flowery language regardless of topic.

You may alter your approach. You may change structure. You may revise vocabulary to suit audience expectations. The underlying voice—your rhythm, your emphasis, your worldview—remains recognizable.

Adjusting Without Overcorrecting

The danger isn't genre itself. The danger is overcorrecting in an effort to fit it.

If you decide that "serious historical writing must sound formal," you may stiffen your prose unnecessarily. If you assume that "business writing must be dry," you may strip out clarity and personality in the name of professionalism. If you believe that "memoir must be lyrical," you may force imagery that doesn't come naturally to you.

Adjustment is part of craft. Overcorrection destroys it.

When you enter a new genre, ask what the reader expects. Then ask what you naturally bring to the page. The intersection of those two answers is where your voice lives.

Consistency Beneath Change

If you write in multiple genres, take a step back and look across them.

Do you consistently favor dialogue and action over extended scenic description? Do you tend to ground ideas in specific examples rather than abstract language? Do even the shallowest characters have moments of self-revelation? Do you keep prose lean and purposeful?

Those through-lines matter more than surface differences.

Genre may shape the presentation, but it does not require you to disappear.

In the next chapter, we'll bring the entire conversation together and talk about sustaining your voice over time—through growth, experimentation, and the inevitable evolution that comes with experience.

Reflection Questions

- What assumptions do you hold about how a particular genre should sound?
- Where might you be overcorrecting in order to fit those expectations?
- What elements of your voice remain consistent across different types of writing?
- If you switched genres tomorrow, what would still sound unmistakably like you?

Exercise

Take one piece of your writing from a genre you're comfortable in. Now imagine writing in a different category—fiction instead of nonfiction, memoir instead of business writing, or vice versa. List what you would need to adjust for reader expectations. Then list what would likely remain the same.

The second list is your anchor.

CHAPTER EIGHT

Your Voice vs. Your Character's

"If I have a strong author voice, won't all my characters sound the same?"

It's a fair concern, but if you understand the distinction between author voice and character voice, you can have strong both.

Your author voice is the consistent narrative fingerprint that runs through your work. It shows up in overall pacing, emphasis, rhythm, and worldview. Character voice, on the other hand, belongs to the individuals inside the story. It governs how they speak, what they notice, and how they interpret events.

Those two layers work together. They are not the same thing.

Author Voice vs. Character Voice

Imagine your book is a building. Your author voice is the foundation, the framework, maybe even the walls. The characters provide everything else: the windows through which the reader sees the world and the décor that makes the building useful and interesting.

If you write with lean, purposeful prose, that clarity may carry through whether your protagonist is sarcastic, solemn, or naïve. If you favor concrete detail over abstract commentary, that tendency will likely appear regardless of which character is narrating.

At the same time, your characters should not all speak with identical rhythms or vocabulary. A teenage protagonist should not sound like a retired professor unless that contrast is deliberate. A hardened detective should not process events the same way as an idealistic intern.

Author voice provides cohesion and structure. Character voice provides variation. In fact, when a character's voice is strong, it might even try to supersede the author. There's a skill in knowing how to maintain balance and when to let go.

Author vs. Character Voice: *Gapman*

For example, I have a first-person fantasy series, *DragonEye, PI*. All the stories are told from the POV of Vern, my snarky dragon detective. His voice is so distinctive that many of his fans treat him as if he were real. They tell me to pass on messages—which he of course, responds to in his own Vernish way.

However, one book was not Vern's story. It introduced Gapman, a human who would accidentally and magically obtain superpowers. Vern got stuck training him up so he didn't cause chaos. Maybe I could have told the whole story from Vern's point of view, but it would not have been nearly as much fun.

Gapman (a.k.a. Ronnie Engleson, mild-mannered entertainment reporter) is about as opposite from Vern as a character can be. He's naïvely optimistic, almost a Pollyanna, where Vern's cynical as only an immortal, superior being can be. Gapman's overeager, while Vern's begrudging. Gapman's default mode is "Wait! What?" while Vern's "Wait—what?" is reserved for moments of ultimate frustration.

The book, *Gapman*, became a duet of their voices, sometimes seeing the same events from two different lenses. It was fun to write, but I had to be careful not to let Vern's strong voice bleed into Ronnie's.

Similarly, I had to watch that my author voice didn't interfere with the fresh-faced baby superhero's. At times, there were jokes I wanted to make but could not because we were in Ronnie's POV and he'd never think something so sardonic or—*gasp*—mean!

Even so, the book fits seamlessly into the series because the foundations were still there: the strong adventure, the humor, both physical and sarcastic (and puns! Vern and Ron both love puns), even the moments of faith that impacted Ron as well, even though he was not religious.

Gapman wove himself so well into the world, keeping his own voice while working within that of the narrator (me), that he's often a side character in subsequent Vern novels, bringing a new dimension of humor and adventure to the series.

The point of this example? A well-developed author voice will have the flexibility to accommodate a strong character voice—and the story will come out even better for it.

First Person vs. Third Person

In first person, the character's internal voice becomes the narrative voice. That means it may overshadow your author voice.

Vern is the narrator of the DragonEye series. He sounds cynical, sarcastic, often annoyed.

> A scarecrow of a human with an ill-fitting uniform and a heavy utility belt that threatened to slide off his hips schlepped his way toward us. He gave me a disinterested look, then handed a paper to Cliffman.

> "Barry Manns reporting for his shift. Can you sign this, so my supervisor knows I'm here?"
>
> With a grin, Cliffman did so, then introduced us. "Vern, Barry here is going to work security for you."
>
> I looked over my guard. Barely Man did not make me feel secure. "Is he protecting me from the humans or vice-versa?"
>
> *Murder Most Picante* by Karina Fabian (2020: Laser Cow Press), page 68

If you're writing in first person, the character's personality must shape diction, rhythm, and focus. However, your authorial tendencies still operate underneath. You still decide what receives emphasis (although always remembering you are in the character's POV). You still control pacing. You may still determine how much description enters the scene—but that can depend on what your character wants or needs, too.

In the case of *DragonEye, PI*, my voice comes through in the descriptions of action, the overall worldview which, despite his cynicism, is generally positive and full of faith and love. It's seen in how others treat him and in how he responds. It's in the vocabulary and sentence structure of the overall narrative, too.

In third person, the separation can feel clearer. The narration may sit slightly outside the character's direct thoughts, allowing your author voice to feel more visible. Yet even in close third person, where we filter events through a specific character's perception, the underlying structure still belongs to you.

The key question is not whether your characters sound different. They should. The key question is whether the book still feels unified.

The Derek Question

Regardless of what person you write in, your characters need their own voices. Sometimes, however, authors use characters as shortcuts for their own words, or simply get sloppy, and that kills the character's voice. Here's a practical test I use when teaching this concept, which we'll call the Derek Question.

If your character, Derek, makes a sarcastic comment, who owns the sarcasm? Is it Genuine Derek? Or are you the narrator putting words into his mouth he might not say? And by "line" I don't just mean dialogue, but also interior thoughts, and even the observations they are making through their own senses.

This was the issue I had with *Gapman*. Sometimes I, the author, saw something I wanted to comment on, but I could not because Ron didn't see it or it was not in his personality to notice or to comment. In that case, I had to sacrifice author voice to keep my character uniquely himself.

There's nothing wrong with narrative commentary. In fact, some genres thrive on it. But you should know when you're doing it.

This test can also be used to check if characters are differentiated. If every character delivers witty asides or heartfelt affirmations or deep philosophical ruminations all in the same rhythm, you may not be differentiating voices enough and quite possibly are falling into author voice. If your reader loses track of the characters, even when they have distinctive names and different appearances, then you may be using your voice and not theirs.

On the other hand, if you remove all narrative personality in an attempt to avoid overlap, you lose the foundation, and chaos ensues. Now your reader lacks a feeling of coherence to ground them in the story.

Ask yourself: Does this line belong to Derek? Or does it belong to me?

Sometimes the answer is "both." That's fine, too. Occasionally, we the author put ourselves into a story. Just be aware when you do this and use it with purpose.

Head Hopping vs. Structured Shifts

Variation strengthens a book when it's intentional.

If you're shifting point of view between characters, the transitions should feel structured rather than accidental. Each viewpoint should carry its own emotional angle and priorities. What the warrior notices may differ from what the scholar notices. What the anxious entrepreneur focuses on will differ from what the confident CEO sees.

Head hopping, however, occurs when the narrative slips between perspectives within a scene without clear structure. The result isn't rich variation. It's confusion.

"Clear structure" has some room for interpretation. As a reader growing up, I read plenty of books where POV flowed from one character to another without scene break or skipped line, especially when writing in the narrator omniscient point of view. By the time I was deep into writing for publication, this was verboten. If you changed character point of view, you skipped a line, used asterisks, or even started a new chapter. Even now, the unmarked POV shift is rare, but I do see it come up now and again.

What makes the difference between smooth transition and abrupt head-hop is how well it's marked and anticipated, and how distinctly you portray the new perspective. That skill will help define your author voice as well.

Consistency in author voice does not require you to stay inside one character's head. It requires you to manage perspective deliberately.

When Variation Strengthens a Book

Novels need variety, contrast, even conflict, that character voice supplies. Different characters can bring distinct diction, humor, or emotional framing to the same event. That variation deepens the world and makes relationships more dynamic.

What Does This Mean for Nonfiction?

You may not have a Derek haunting the pages of your academic treatise of science fiction (unless it's *The Orville*; then there's always a Derek). However, you may have character-like variations in your prose.

In memoir, for example, you may shift between your present reflective voice and your younger lived voice. In a business book, you may alternate between analytical explanation and anecdotal storytelling. Those shifts can add texture, as long as they remain anchored in a consistent overall tone.

Variation strengthens a book when it clarifies perspective.

However, just like fiction writers need to avoid head-hopping, nonfiction writers need to make sure they treat changes in narrative voice carefully. If your narration begins in a restrained, measured tone and suddenly erupts into slang-heavy commentary without narrative justification, readers feel the jolt. If you move from conversational to academic mid-chapter without signaling the shift, readers feel distance.

Jarring shifts can happen when writers experiment without fully integrating the change into their established voice. Sometimes, they occur because time away from the draft means you've lost track of the approach in previous chapters.

It can help to go back and re-read, but if you are raring to go full-speed ahead, I suggest just going for it. Edits are the optimal time to check for issues or inconsistencies. Just be sure not to edit so much you lose the energy of your unique voice.

Consistency does not mean monotony. It means cohesion.

Now that we've addressed how genre and character affect voice, let's talk about how time can affect it.

Reflection Questions

- When you read your dialogue aloud, do your characters sound like distinct individuals—or like variations of the same narrator?
- In first-person scenes, can you clearly separate what belongs to the character's worldview from what belongs to your authorial perspective?
- When you shift between characters or viewpoints, does the emotional focus change naturally, or does the tone remain identical?
- Are there moments where your narration slips into commentary that doesn't fully belong to the point-of-view character? Is that intentional?
- Across different characters, does your underlying pacing, clarity, and emphasis remain consistent—even as their personalities differ?

Exercise

Choose a simple scene—two characters in conversation, or a brief moment of conflict.

First, write it from one character's perspective. Let their personality shape diction and focus.

Then rewrite the same scene from the other character's perspective.

Now compare the two versions. The character voices should differ in what they notice and how they interpret events. At the same time, the pacing, clarity, and overall tone should still feel like the same author wrote both.

If the two versions feel like they belong in entirely different books, examine why. Did your author voice disappear? Or did you successfully create variation within cohesion?

CHAPTER NINE

As Your Voice Evolves

We've talked a lot about developing your author voice. You've done exercises, reflected on questions, maybe even analyzed your writing and that of others. If you have a good handle on your voice—bravo! But remember one thing:

All that will change.

That's kind of exciting, really. As you grow in your craft, your voice will mature, expand, and encounter new angles and aspects you never expected. You'll be ready for new challenges, and those challenges in turn will impact your voice.

How My Voice Has Grown

I've been writing *DragonEye, PI* stories since 2008, but around 2018, I decided to reboot the series. One of the things I did was expand the short story "Mishmash" into a novel. It's the story of how Vern met Sister Grace, a nun mage, and brought her into his detective business with him. Expansion aside, look at the difference ten years made to the same scene: Vern meets Grace.

Old:

> **Wednesday**
>
> I looked up from the sheet of music Sister Grace had set on my desk and regarded the Faerie nun thoughtfully. Human, her Irish blood telling in her pale skin and bone structure. Eyes the color of the Mediterranean on a peaceful afternoon. She sat straight and solid in my cheap folding chair, her hands placidly in her lap. A human would see the picture of calm, but my other senses told me that she wanted nothing more than an excuse to set fire to this particular sheet of music, if only she could guarantee that would erase all traces of it from the Mundane universe.

I wondered if she would turn on me if I gave her an answer she didn't want to hear. Religious or not, her habit was that of an order of mages, and she was a nun on the edge.

She couldn't kill me, of course, but I had no doubt she could severely inconvenience me for a few decades.

Now, the 2018 version:

I used my 270-degree vision to get a more complete look at Sister Grace than I had while distracted by children. She was average for a Faerie human, five-two, maybe 140 pounds. A good amount of muscle, but enough fat to tell me she ate well and had probably been on a Mundane cuisine for at least a year. I felt a pang of envy. Wish I had enough food to fatten myself up. Her face looked pleasant enough, except that it was pinched with stress. All of her muscles were tight. I could feel waves to tension flowing off her.

That wasn't what caught my attention the most, however. It was the magic flowing around her, hesitant and held at bay. Most mages, most Magicals, took in at least a small wisp of magic. It was so commonplace, I didn't notice. Grace was at

> once attracting magic and pushing it away, and the effect struck my senses like air with too much static…
>
> *Nun of My Business* by Karina Fabian (2022: Laser Cow Press), page 28

Now, some of the difference is novel vs. short story, but notice the way he recognizes the dangerous aspects of her. In the first story, he notes her tension, makes an assumption about her wanting to set fire to the music, and assesses how dangerous she is. In the later version, there's more analysis—not just tight muscles but he feels the tension and even more the ominous push and pull of magic around her—which, incidentally, foreshadows her inner conflict that was resolved in both versions.

This was the direct result of practicing to show more than tell and of learning to get more deeply into Vern's head to not just see what he sees but feel what he feels, even with senses I don't possess.

Even so, you could read either tale and know it was Vern telling the story and me writing it.

There's still his sardonic humor and me-first attitude. The description is purposeful. The focus stays on character over scenery. The structure is tight. What changed was depth and execution, not identity.

Maturity Adds Layers

Ogres have layers—and so does voice! As you continue writing, you begin to see more in your own scenes.

Early in a writing career, it can be an accomplishment simply to move the plot forward clearly. Dialogue works—check! Action makes sense—yep! The scene lands where it's supposed to land—huzzah! That's no small accomplishment.

Over time, however, you start to ask different questions. What is this character not saying? What tension lies under the surface? What emotional thread can be woven more subtly into the description? How can this moment carry meaning beyond the immediate action?

That shift does not replace your voice. It enriches it.

If you naturally lean toward humor, maturity won't remove that humor. It may give it sharper timing or deeper contrast. If you prefer tight prose, growth may not make you suddenly lush and descriptive. Rather, that maturing voice may make you more precise about the details you choose and help you see where your story could benefit from an expanded emotional beat or a deeper layer of sensory detail.

The instinct stays. The control improves.

Expanding Your Range

You may also find that your range expands.

Perhaps you once wrote only lighthearted stories and later felt drawn to more serious themes. Perhaps you began in nonfiction and discovered that fiction allowed you to explore ideas more freely. Perhaps you experimented with a different age group or genre and found new strengths.

That happened to me in 2024-2025. After nearly three decades of writing science fiction and fantasy aimed at adults, I not only ventured into middle-grade sci-fi but also wrote a serious family drama about addiction and a failed marriage. The middle-grade book, *Zach Augustine in Stowaway to Saturn*, is my first sale to a major publisher, and the drama is being considered by an agent as I write this book. And now, I'm writing books on writing!

I've known other authors who have expanded their literary reach. Jane Lebak moved from science fiction/fantasy to cozy romance. Fiction writer Larry Correia published a hard-hitting, deeply researched and thought-out book on the Second Amendment. Joseph Pearce, who wrote the autobiography *Race with the Devil,* normally publishes academic analyses of literature and literary figures.

Broadening your scope, even into radically different genres, does not mean abandoning your voice. Rather, it's the uniqueness of your voice that enables you to give your own distinctive contribution to a new genre.

Depth Takes Practice

What changed between the two versions of Vern meeting Grace was not inspiration. It was practice.

I learned to trust subtext more. I learned to filter experience more completely through character perspective. I learned to let tension exist in sensory detail rather than naming it outright.

Those skills came from writing, revising, analyzing, and writing again.

Your voice will deepen the same way.

The more you write, the more you'll start to sense when a scene is stopping too soon. The more you read, the more you'll recognize emotional beats and see how they play out in your own works. The more critique and feedback you get, the more you discover the times that you are explaining something the reader could infer.

That awareness is growth.

You do not need to chase evolution. It happens with the work of writing. In the final chapter, we'll talk a little about that and wrap up with some final thoughts.

Reflection Questions

- When you compare an older piece of your writing to something recent, what differences do you notice in depth or execution?
- What elements have remained consistent across time?
- In what areas has your craft improved through deliberate practice?
- Have you allowed your voice to expand naturally, or are you trying to control it too tightly?
- What challenge might help stretch your voice in healthy ways without forcing artificial change?

CHAPTER TEN

Want Voice? Write!

After all the exercises, comparisons, reflection questions, and analysis, developing voice comes down to one thing.

You have to write.

There is no shortcut around that reality. You can study voice. You can admire it in other authors. You can analyze it in your own work. All of that helps, but voice does not fully take shape until you accumulate pages. It becomes clear through repetition, through patterns that reveal themselves over time, and through steady practice.

If you want a confident voice, you need material to work with.

Voice Emerges Through Volume

If you're a beginning writer and still aren't sure about your voice, don't worry. Patterns only become visible across distance. A single paragraph may not reveal much. A single chapter may still feel experimental. But across multiple stories, essays, articles, or books, your tendencies become unmistakable.

You begin to see where you naturally slow down and where you move quickly. You notice how often you rely on dialogue, reflection, or concrete sensory detail. You recognize the tonal thread that runs beneath different genres or formats.

That clarity comes from volume.

This is why the "one million words" advice persists. The number itself is less important than the principle behind it. The early words are not wasted. They are training. They are where you stretch, overreach, experiment, and occasionally fall flat. They are where you begin to separate what feels authentic from what feels borrowed—or where you make what was borrowed into something uniquely you.

If you keep writing long enough, your voice stops feeling accidental and starts feeling deliberate.

You Can't Polish a Blank Page

Writers sometimes hesitate when writing the first draft because they want the voice to sound right from the beginning. That instinct is understandable, but it is also counterproductive.

While it's true that your voice comes out when you are relaxed in your writing and not thinking about editing, revision is where you can sharpen it and make it shine.

Regardless, you can't get there until you write. Revision requires substance. You cannot refine what does not exist. A draft may be uneven. It may overexplain. It may shift tone awkwardly. That is part of the process.

When you produce pages consistently, you give yourself something to improve. You begin to see where your natural voice is strongest and where it needs support from craft. You can adjust pacing, trim excess, deepen emotional beats, and strengthen clarity. None of that happens in theory. It happens on the page.

If you want to hear your voice clearly, you must first let it speak imperfectly.

Growth Through Experiment and Play

Whether you are just beginning to find your voice or you're looking for ways to develop it further, I encourage you to experiment. Play. Writing should be fun.

Try a different tense or point of view. Write something darker than usual or lighter than your typical tone. Take a stab at nonfiction if you primarily write fiction, or explore fiction if you usually write essays or articles. Try out a different age category or genre to see what stretches you.

Do it without pressure. Perhaps your writing group can challenge each other with an assignment. Or take a webinar on writing something outside your comfort zone.

If pressure motivates you, find an assignment that pays or publishes. I like to write for anthologies, and some of those stories have directly led not just to novels, but whole series.

Some experiments will confirm your strengths. Others will show you what does not fit. Either way, you'll learn what is foundational and what was simply fun.

Permission to Refine

As your awareness increases, refinement becomes more intentional.

If you know you lean toward sparse descriptions and action, growth probably won't turn you into a Tolkienesque worldbuilder. Instead, that maturing voice inspires you to add more applicable details that propel the story forward. You do not abandon restraint; you apply it more skillfully.

If humor is natural to you, refinement may help you control its timing so that it enhances rather than undercuts tension. If you prefer analysis in nonfiction, refinement may help you balance clarity with narrative illustration.

Refinement is not self-erasure. It is strengthening what is already yours.

Grow Without Forcing It

You do not need to chase evolution. It happens.

Keep writing. Keep reflecting. Keep studying what works and what does not. Seek feedback when appropriate. Try new challenges. Allow yourself to be stretched by projects that demand more of you.

At the same time, resist the urge to reinvent yourself simply because you think you should sound more sophisticated or more marketable. Growth is not about discarding what made your writing recognizable in the first place. It is about strengthening it.

If you look back ten years from now and see improvement, that is not a betrayal of your earlier voice. It is evidence that you stayed with the craft long enough to mature. And if readers can still recognize you beneath that growth, you have done it well.

Confidence Without Arrogance

There have been times when as an editor or a critiquer, I've made suggestions or highlighted something that doesn't work, and the response back was, "Well, that's my style."

If your style confuses your reader, your story fails. If you hide behind style to avoid making edits, you fail your story. Knowing your style does not mean declaring it superior or refusing to learn.

You do not need to mimic someone else to be legitimate, and you do not need to chase every trend to remain relevant. At the same time, you should remain open to correction, attentive to craft, and mindful of your readers.

Confidence says, "This is how I naturally tell a story," but it also says, "I am willing to improve."

That balance is sustainable.

Keep Going

There is no final moment when your voice is complete. It continues to develop as long as you continue to write. That's what keeps writing fresh year after year.

Even so, if you want a voice that is steady, recognizable, and mature, the path is not mysterious. It is steady work over time. It is permission to experiment and discipline to refine. It is growth without panic and confidence without rigidity.

Most of all, it is persistence.

Write. Then write more.

The Write Boost

Practical Writing and Marketing Guides for Growing Writers

The Write Boost: Practical Writing and Marketing Guides for Growing Writers is a series of short, focused eBooks designed to help beginning and early-intermediate writers strengthen their writing craft and build real momentum. Each volume tackles one essential skill—from worldbuilding to editing, goal-setting to critique groups, idea generation to author marketing—with clear instruction, real examples, and practical exercises you can use right away.

Written by award-winning author Karina Fabian, these guides combine decades of professional experience, honest lessons learned, and a healthy dose of encouragement. You don't have to master everything at once. Just pick the boost you need, apply it, and keep moving forward.

KEEP IN TOUCH

If you want to learn about future books, please

- Sign up for my newsletter. https://fabianspace.substack.com/subscribe Get short stories, updates, and a free book!
- Visit my website at https://karinafabian.com
- Follow me on Facebook: https://www.facebook.com/Karina-Fabian-Speculative-Fiction-with-a-Grin-2233839790277963

ABOUT THE AUTHOR

Karina Fabian is an award-winning novelist, speaker, and stand-up comedian who has spent decades telling stories in as many ways as she can manage, from space-faring nuns to dragon private investigators. She's written over 50 science fiction and fantasy novels, plus short stories and humorous works.

In addition to writing fiction, she teaches workshops and webinars for beginning writers, sharing the lessons she's learned through success, trial and error, and stubborn perseverance. She believes you can take the craft seriously without taking yourself too seriously—and that writing is at its best when skill, heart, and a little bit of laughter work together.

Karina lives on Merritt Island with her husband, two of her four kids, two dogs, and a menagerie of imaginary friends who all want to tell her their stories.

THERE'S MORE FUN IN FABIANSPACE!

Science Fiction

Space Traipse: Hold My Beer: Redneck ingenuity and common sense in a Star Trek-ish universe. Enjoy the adventures of the *HMB Impulsive*.

The Rescue Sisters: Intrepid women doing dangerous missions in space for the love of God and humankind.

The Old Man and the Void: Dex hunts relics on the edge of the black hole, and bags the catch of a lifetime.

Jovian Heat: As the next Great Storm of Jupiter rises, Cass must find the father of a baby in peril—but the father died before the child was conceived.

Fantasy

DragonEye Story: Vern's a snarky dragon on the wrong side of the Interdimensional Gap, solving crimes, battling evil, and saving the universes on an all-too-regular basis.

Madness of Kanaan: Deryl isn't crazy; he's psychic, and aliens of two worlds thinks he can save them. Maybe he can—but can he regain his sanity in the process?

Horror

Neeta Lyffe, Zombie Exterminator: Neeta's an average exterminator, taking out bugs, rodents, and the undead. Can she keep her friends alive, pay her bills, and find romance?

Frightliner and Other Tales of the Supernatural (with Colleen Drippé): Truck-driving vampires terrorizing the road, Southern women doing what needs doing, a zombie wedding—a great story collection for horror lovers.

www.ingramcontent.com/pod-product-compliance
Lightning Source LLC
LaVergne TN
LVHW010949110826
845149LV00015B/3271

* 9 7 8 1 9 5 6 4 8 9 2 8 6 *